DATE			

VENUS
WILLIAMS

VENUS WILLIAMS

Sandy Asirvatham

CHELSEA HOUSE PUBLISHERS
Philadelphia

Chelsea House Publishers

Editor in Chief	Sally Cheney
Director of Production	Kim Shinners
Production Manager	Pamela Loos
Art Director	Sara Davis
Production Editor	Diann Grasse

Staff for VENUS WILLIAMS

Senior Editor	LeeAnne Gelletly
Associate Editor	Brian Baughan
Associate Art Director	Takeshi Takahashi
Layout	21st Century Publishing and Communications

The Chelsea House World Wide Web address is
http://www.chelseahouse.com

3 5 7 9 8 6 4 2

Library of Congress Cataloging-in-Publication Data

Asirvatham, Sandy.
Venus Williams / Sandy Asirvatham.
     p.   cm. — (Black Americans of Achievement)
Includes bibliographical references (p.   ) and index
Summary: A biography of the young tennis player who has been ranked among
the top ten women players in the world.
ISBN 0-7910-6289-9 (alk. paper) — ISBN 0-7910-6290-2 (pbk.: alk. paper)
1. Williams, Venus, 1980—Juvenile literature. 2. Tennis players—United States
—Biography—Juvenile literature. 3. African American women tennis players—
Biography—Juvenile literature. [1. Williams, Venus, 1980- 2. Tennis players.
3. Women—Biography. 4. African Americans—Biography.] I. Title. II.Series.

GV994.W49 A85 2001
796.342'092—dc21
[B]   2001042098

Frontispiece:
*Venus Williams, one of the
most powerful forces in
women's tennis, prepares to
deliver a blistering serve.*

CONTENTS

BLACK AMERICANS OF ACHIEVEMENT

HENRY AARON
baseball great

KAREEM ABDUL-JABBAR
basketball great

MUHAMMAD ALI
heavyweight champion

RICHARD ALLEN
religious leader and social activist

MAYA ANGELOU
author

LOUIS ARMSTRONG
musician

ARTHUR ASHE
tennis great

JOSEPHINE BAKER
entertainer

TYRA BANKS
model

BENJAMIN BANNEKER
scientist and mathematician

COUNT BASIE
bandleader and composer

ANGELA BASSETT
actress

ROMARE BEARDEN
artist

HALLE BERRY
actress

MARY MCLEOD BETHUNE
educator

GEORGE WASHINGTON
CARVER
botanist

JOHNNIE COCHRAN
lawyer

BILL COSBY
entertainer

MILES DAVIS
musician

FREDERICK DOUGLASS
abolitionist editor

CHARLES DREW
physician

PAUL LAURENCE DUNBAR
poet

DUKE ELLINGTON
bandleader and composer

RALPH ELLISON
author

JULIUS ERVING
basketball great

LOUIS FARRAKHAN
political activist

ELLA FITZGERALD
singer

ARETHA FRANKLIN
entertainer

MORGAN FREEMAN
actor

MARCUS GARVEY
black nationalist leader

JOSH GIBSON
baseball great

WHOOPI GOLDBERG
entertainer

DANNY GLOVER
actor

CUBA GOODING JR.
actor

ALEX HALEY
author

PRINCE HALL
social reformer

JIMI HENDRIX
musician

MATTHEW HENSON
explorer

GREGORY HINES
performer

BILLIE HOLIDAY
singer

LENA HORNE
entertainer

WHITNEY HOUSTON
singer and actress

LANGSTON HUGHES
poet

JANET JACKSON
musician

JESSE JACKSON
civil-rights leader and politician

MICHAEL JACKSON
entertainer

SAMUEL L. JACKSON
actor

T. D. JAKES
religious leader

JACK JOHNSON
heavyweight champion

MAE JEMISON
astronaut

MAGIC JOHNSON
basketball great

SCOTT JOPLIN
composer

BARBARA JORDAN
politician

MICHAEL JORDAN
basketball great

CORETTA SCOTT KING
civil-rights leader

MARTIN LUTHER KING, JR.
civil-rights leader

LEWIS LATIMER
scientist

SPIKE LEE
filmmaker

CARL LEWIS
champion athlete

RONALD McNAIR
astronaut

MALCOLM X
militant black leader

BOB MARLEY
musician

THURGOOD MARSHALL
Supreme Court justice

TERRY McMILLAN
author

TONI MORRISON
author

ELIJAH MUHAMMAD
religious leader

EDDIE MURPHY
entertainer

JESSE OWENS
champion athlete

SATCHEL PAIGE
baseball great

CHARLIE PARKER
musician

ROSA PARKS
civil-rights leader

COLIN POWELL
military leader

QUEEN LATIFAH
entertainer

DELLA REESE
entertainer

PAUL ROBESON
singer and actor

JACKIE ROBINSON
baseball great

CHRIS ROCK
comedian and actor

DIANA ROSS
entertainer

AL SHARPTON
minister and activist

WILL SMITH
actor

WESLEY SNIPES
actor

CLARENCE THOMAS
Supreme Court justice

SOJOURNER TRUTH
antislavery activist

HARRIET TUBMAN
antislavery activist

NAT TURNER
slave revolt leader

TINA TURNER
entertainer

ALICE WALKER
author

MADAM C. J. WALKER
entrepreneur

BOOKER T. WASHINGTON
educator

DENZEL WASHINGTON
actor

J. C. WATTS
politician

VANESSA WILLIAMS
singer and actress

VENUS WILLIAMS
tennis star

OPRAH WINFREY
entertainer

TIGER WOODS
golf star

ON ACHIEVEMENT

❦

Coretta Scott King

Before you begin this book, I hope you will ask yourself what the word *excellence* means to you. I think it's a question we should all ask, and keep asking as we grow older and change. Because the truest answer to it should never change. When you think of excellence, perhaps you think of success at work; or of becoming wealthy; or meeting the right person, getting married, and having a good family life.

Those goals are worth striving for, but there is a better way to look at excellence. As Martin Luther King Jr. said in one of his last sermons, "I want you to be first in love. I want you to be first in moral excellence. I want you to be first in generosity. If you want to be important, wonderful. If you want to be great, wonderful. But recognize that he who is greatest among you shall be your servant."

My husband knew that the true meaning of achievement is service. When I met him, in 1952, he was already ordained as a Baptist minister and was working toward a doctoral degree at Boston University. I was studying at the New England Conservatory and dreamed of accomplishments in music. We married a year later, and after I graduated the following year we moved to Montgomery, Alabama. We didn't know it then, but our notions of achievement were about to undergo a dramatic change.

You may have read or heard about what happened next. What began with the boycott of a local bus line grew into a national crusade, and by the time he was assassinated in 1968 my husband had fashioned a black movement powerful enough to shatter forever the practice of racial segregation. What you may not have read about is where he learned to resist injustice without compromising his religious beliefs.

He adopted a strategy of nonviolence from a man of a different race, who lived in a different country and even practiced a different religion. The man was Mahatma Gandhi, the great leader of India, who devoted his life to serving humanity in the spirit of love and nonviolence. It was in these principles that Martin discovered his method for social reform. More than anything else, those two principles were the key to his achievements.

These books are about African Americans who served society through the excellence of their achievements. They form part of the rich history of black men and women in America—a history of stunning accomplishments in every field of human endeavor, from literature and art to science, industry, education, diplomacy, athletics, jurisprudence, even polar exploration.

Not all of the people in this history had the same ideals, but I think you will find that all of them had something in common. Like Martin Luther King Jr., they all decided to become "drum majors" and serve humanity. In that principle—whether it was expressed in books, inventions, or song—they found a goal and a guide outside themselves that showed them a way to serve others instead of living only for themselves.

Reading the stories of these courageous men and women not only helps us discover the principles that we will use to guide our own lives; it also teaches us about our black heritage and about America itself. It is crucial for us to know the heroes and heroines of our history and to realize that the price we paid in our struggle for equality in America was dear. But we must also understand that we have gotten as far as we have partly because America's democratic system and ideals made it possible.

We are still struggling with racism and prejudice. But the great men and women in this series are a tribute to the spirit of the country in which they have flourished. And that makes their stories special and worth knowing.

1

A STAR FROM THE START

⚬⚬

IT WAS THE spring of 1991. A girl sat in the living room of her family's house in a Los Angeles ghetto, fidgeting, but trying to be polite while an adult guest asked her questions. This guest was not simply one of her parents' friends making her acquaintance for the first time, or a teacher discussing her academic performance, or neighbor who'd come over for a visit. This was a reporter from a famous national magazine called *Sports Illustrated*, on assignment to interview a very young, very talented legend-in-the-making: Venus Williams, an African-American 5th-grader who got straight A's, liked to play tag and hide-and-seek, wore her hair in cornrows or dangling braids, and was already a celebrity tennis player with an eye toward a professional athletic career—although her back-up choices were to become an archaeologist or an astronaut.

She was only 10 years and 11 months old. But she answered the reporter's questions with the poise and self-assurance of an athlete twice her age, as if she'd been born to be interviewed—born, in other words, to be famous.

Television usually bored her, she said, but she always watched if there was a tennis match on. "I try to see if they're playing smart and concentrating, and playing to their opponents' weaknesses.

Venus Williams rejoices after her championship victory over Jennifer Capriati in the 2001 Ericsson Open in Key Biscayne, Florida.

That's what I try to do when I play." Known as an unusually aggressive player for one so young, she described her own approach to the game with an intimidating level of strategic understanding and self-confidence. "If you give me a short shot, I will attack you. I'm not a baseliner who rallies. I try to get the point over with."

Venus had yet to achieve her full adult height of 6' 1", and it would be a few years still before she'd start hitting her record-breaking serves of over 120 mph. But at 10 she was already a 5' 4" tower of power, speed, and skill—the number one ranked player in Southern California in the girls' 12-and-under division. Because of her height and her abilities, older tennis pros sometimes assumed she was 14 or 15 when they first witnessed her playing at various celebrity or charity tournaments featuring child players. Zina Garrison, a 1990 Wimbledon finalist and one of the few African-American tennis players ever to achieve national ranking, met Venus at an anti-drug celebrity tournament in October 1990. "For 10 years old, Venus is exceptional," Garrison said at the time. "She would have beaten the 10-year-old Zina into the ground."

But beyond her precocious level of athletic ability, Venus Williams was destined to gain a following for a number of other reasons.

Until rather recently in history, tennis had been a "country club" sport, an exclusive endeavor for the rich, wealthy, white folks who belonged to the race- and class-restricted private clubs where the game was taught and played. This situation changed over time, and with the beginning of professional "open tennis" in the late 1960s, it become theoretically possible for anyone to learn the game, excel at it if they had the talent and the drive, and rise to national-level rankings.

But the fact remains that most people who have

achieved greatness in tennis have come from the middle- and upper-classes, from families that can afford the lessons and tournament fees and, perhaps, coaching sessions with famous ex-professionals who charge several hundred dollars an hour. Or else, even if they aren't particularly well-to-do, they may have a "legacy" in the sport—their father or mother played the game, and has become their primary teacher, coach, and mentor.

They do not normally come from a burned-out, gang-ruled neighborhood of South Central Los Angeles. They do not normally have to worry about gunfire, or practice with old balls on the broken glass-covered neighborhood courts, as Venus Williams did. They have not normally been coached by a father who taught himself tennis from books and instructional videos, as Venus Williams was coached.

At the start of the 1990s, much of the attention showered upon the 10-year-old tennis prodigy— as well as upon her 9-year-old sister, Serena, who was the top-ranked girl in the Southern California 10-and-under division at the time—was due, quite simply, to notable athletic gifts. But in a country that believes fervently in rags-to-riches stories, Venus was the complete package. No wonder *Sports Illustrated* wanted to profile her. She was a genuine talent about to embark on a fairy-tale life—an inspiration to poor but ambitious youngsters everywhere. She was the "Cinderella of the ghetto," as her father eventually came to call her.

Has Venus Williams lived up to the early hype? Ten years later, by the beginning of a new century and new millennium, both Venus and her younger sister, Serena, had become bona fide tennis champs. By the ages of 20 and 19, Venus and Serena —sometimes opponents, sometimes doubles part- ners, but always close friends—were ranked respectively as the third and sixth world's best players among women tennis professionals.

The promise seen a decade earlier in a gangly, aggressive 10-year-old player was becoming a reality. True, Venus hadn't lived up to some of her bolder ambitions, such as being ranked number one in professional tennis by the age of 18. At 20, she still had much to learn about the nuances of competitive tennis and was only at about 75 percent of her playing ability, according to her mentor, tennis great Billie Jean King. But as of the beginning of the new millennium she had had a remarkable career, and was already talking about her eventual retirement and the next highly competitive occupation she wanted to conquer: the fashion design business.

In January 2001, the sisters—now old pros at interviews—were the subject of a cover story in a glossy national women's magazine, *Elle*. The writer, Devin Friedman, began his article by admitting he was a bit intimidated to meet the Williams sisters, who play so powerfully and "have a reputation on tour for being haughty and reticent." Then he went on to discuss the various facts that make them "outsiders" in the world of tennis, despite their fame and professional success.

> They didn't learn the game at a country club and later hang out with all the other girls at junior tournaments; [they] are black in a sport where practically no one else is black; they are flamboyant in a sport where almost no one else is flamboyant; they're muscular and powerful and compelling in a thousand different ways that tennis has never seen.

But what really sets them apart, Friedman wrote, is that "whenever tennis has deigned to invite them to be like everyone else . . . the sisters have always famously declined."

Witty and charming some days, moody or arrogant other days, Venus has always remained true

Venus Williams didn't learn tennis at a country club but at this community court in Compton, a rough neighborhood of Los Angeles, California.

to herself, even if that means offending people or going against the mainstream expectations of the sport. She has not changed her personality to suit tennis etiquette, for example, by being friendly to her competitors just because that's what all the other women players do. She may be a kind of "Cinderella," an outsider allowed to attend the

Using her long arms to her advantage, Venus Williams reaches for a shot during a quarterfinal match of the 2001 Australian Open.

insider's party, but Venus has never donned a ball gown and glass slippers and pretended to be something she isn't. Instead, she has changed the game—both how it's played, and how it's perceived by fans and supporters—to fit who she already is.

As a result, rather than being outsiders, Venus and her kid sister Serena have become "the new tennis establishment"—at least according to Devin Friedman and a few other observers who've made similar statements. From now on, it seems that everyone else in the tennis world "is going to have to start being like them."

2

THE BIRTH OF A DREAM

T HE STORY OF Venus Williams can't be understood without first knowing the story of her father, Richard, and how he passed his dreams and ambitions on to his daughter.

He was one of five children—the only boy—of Julia Williams, a single mother in the predominantly black Cedar Grove section of Shreveport, Louisiana. "My mother was my dad, my psychiatrist, my hero, the greatest person who ever lived," he has said. "She taught me pride, decency, religion, and that civilization would disappear when the family went back." Julia eked out a living the traditional way hundreds of thousands of poor blacks had done in the Deep South since the abolition of slavery: by picking cotton. Young Richard saw and participated in this back-breaking, dead-end work, which must have sparked a tremendous desire in him to find a better life.

While finishing high school, Richard worked odd jobs before and after classes to bring money in for the family. After graduation, he moved to Chicago and worked for a number of years in construction, and then moved on to California, to the often-troubled Watts section of Los Angeles. He intended to go to college, but instead he found himself drawn to becoming his own boss, as soon as it was possible. After a stint as a factory laborer, he established a security guard company in Watts, called Samson

Venus (left) and Serena (right) pose with their father, Richard Williams, near the community court where they developed their game.

19

Security. As most entrepreneurs will do, he also tried other businesses at the same time, including a phone-book delivery service.

At church he met a nurse named Oracene Price, originally from Saginaw, Michigan, who went by the nickname Brandi. A lovely, intelligent, family-oriented woman, Oracene became Richard's wife in 1972. The first three Williams daughters—Yetunde, Isha, and Lyndrea—followed soon thereafter.

Williams had been a gifted athlete in school, participating in basketball, football, and golf, but avoiding tennis, which he considered a "sissy game." As the often-told family legend has it, Williams was watching a women's tennis tournament on TV one afternoon, when he happened to catch a glimpse of sports announcer Bud Collins presenting the winner, Virginia Ruzici, with a $30,000 check. "That's what I earn in a year! Let's put our kids in tennis so they can become millionaires," he recalls telling Oracene. It was the late 1970s. Venus and Serena hadn't been born yet.

Many people vow to teach themselves things—a foreign language, a musical instrument—but few actually manage to get past the first few lessons before giving up. It takes a tremendous amount of inner strength and self-direction to master a new pursuit without a school or teacher to provide struc-ture and guidance. Put another way, most people have ambitions that outstrip their ability to stay focused. Richard Williams is a rare exception. With the dream of raising a family of female tennis stars, he taught himself the game using books and instruc-tional videos, and practicing every morning with a group of neighborhood men. They played on a court that sat just 100 yards from the place where the 1965 Watts riots had begun. He collected old tennis balls and eventually had about 550 of them, which he loaded into an old shopping cart in the back of his Volkswagon van.

Having acquired the rudiments of the game, Richard then taught his wife and his three daughters how to play. Years later, he would note that the older three girls were all athletically gifted and showed a lot of promise. But they never fell in love with the game. Ultimately, Yetunde, Isha, and Lyndrea all decided to pursue other paths in life—Yetunda and Lyndrea in medicine and Isha in law.

Venus, born in 1980, was another story altogether, and so was her "baby sis" Serena, born fifteen months later in 1981. From the earliest ages, they had both the talent and the required dedication to the sport. Richard began giving lessons to Venus when she was four, and Serena joined them the following year.

"The first time I knew Venus was going to be a good tennis player was the first time I took her out on her very first day," Richard once told a magazine reporter. With his older daughters losing interest in tennis, he had become the coach for neighborhood kids who wanted to learn the game. These teenagers used to take a very long time hitting all 550 balls that Richard had loaded in his shopping cart.

> They wanted to take breaks. Well, while they were taking a break, Venus wanted to hit every ball in that basket. She wouldn't stop. Every time you tried to stop her, she would start crying. She was only 4 years old. That doesn't mean she hit every ball. A lot of them she missed. But she would swing at every ball. When she got to the last ball in the basket, she told me to say, 'Last one,' and I said, 'Okay, last one.'

Most afternoons, Richard, Venus, and Serena made their way from the small, mint-green, graffiti-painted house they called home to the glass-strewn, unkempt public courts in East Rancho Dominguez, in a neighborhood dominated by drug dealers. Richard jokingly called the courts the "East Compton Hills

Country Club." The trio had even been shot at, although within a few months, the local thugs learned to respect the Williams family and generally stayed out of their way. In what must have been a rather surreal moment of gallantry, some gang members even took it upon themselves to teach Venus and Serena how to drop to the ground and crawl toward safe cover in the event of gunfire.

At a young age, Venus demonstrated all-around athletic gifts similar to her father's. In elementary school, she was undefeated in 19 track meets as both a sprinter and middle-distance runner. At the age of eight, she clocked a speedy 5:29 mile. Richard wanted her to pursue both tennis and track, but Oracene was worried that this would put too much strain on Venus's young body, and asked her to focus on just one. "It will be hard to oblige Venus with all the things she'd like to do, because she's good at so many," Richard said at the time.

Once she chose to concentrate on tennis, Venus became a local hero in no time. By the time she was ten, older ball girls and ball boys at tennis clubs wanted her to sign her autograph to their T-shirts, even though she had only just learned how to write in cursive. Manufacturers sent her clothes, shoes, and tennis rackets. Sports promoter Don King showed up to the Williams house in a limo and took everyone— Venus, her sisters, and her parents—to an L.A. soul-food restaurant for lunch. Sports reporters and agents started calling so often that the family instituted a few new rules. The first was that no one could answer the telephone before 10 A.M. (to maintain the quiet and privacy of mornings). The second was that Venus and Serena were not allowed to tell anyone where they went to elementary school.

Compton had long been burned in the public's imagination as a terrible place to grow up. It was, as one writer described it, "the district of South Central Los Angeles known to most Americans as the 'hood

(as in [the John Singleton film] *Boyz N the . . .*)."
It was not the kind of neighborhood you'd expect a
tennis star to have grown up in. Richard recalled one
time when Venus competed in a tennis tournament
in a snooty Southern California club. "I overheard
some people say we shouldn't even be there. 'They
are from Compton. What are they doing here? They
can't play.'"

Years later, when his years of dreaming and coaching and encouragement had paid off in the form of two
top-ranked tennis playing daughters, Richard made it
a point to let the world know that good, solid families
like his lived and thrived in Compton, along with
the gangs and drug dealers. This idea became a funda-
mental part of the family's inspiring rags-to-riches
story. Although they eventually moved to Florida so
that Venus and Serena could attend a famous tennis
academy there, Richard never renounced his roots.
Along with his strong relationships with his wife and

*Serena (left) and Venus (right),
who have been hitting partners
for over a decade, shake hands
at the net after a friendly game.*

Richard Williams coaches a young Venus from the baseline of the court. During those training years, Richard encouraged both of his tennis-playing daughters to not only excel athletically but also academically.

daughters, it was his close connection to the African-American community there that enabled him to keep pursuing his dreams. When Venus won important matches, Richard would say, "Today was a good day for the ghetto."

From the start, Richard was criticized for believing that he could produce champion-level players on his own with no formal tennis training. Once Venus and Serena began competing in children's tournaments in southern California, people began to notice them for their strength, size, and skill. But even when famous tennis teachers, promoters, and agents approached the family with offers, Richard stuck to his own timetable and his own way of doing things.

He and Oracene said no to people offering houses, cars, and millions of dollars in endorsement deals. He shrugged when he was told that his daughters, no matter how talented, couldn't hope to become competitive without receiving training from a professional. He took flak from sports commentators who believed that "women's" tennis had become overly obsessed with promoting its youngest stars, who weren't even teenagers yet, let alone women. He still received criticism when he decided to pull Venus off the junior tournament circuit for three years when she was eleven years old.

The plan was to allow Venus to practice, improve, and prepare for a professional career, without the immediate pressure of competition. It was also important to Richard that Venus spend some time concentrating on her school work, for he had every intention of sending her to college. In Richard's view of the world, tennis was a good first career for his girls, but no amount of success in sports could ever take the place of a solid education. On another level, Richard was also trying to protect his daughter from having to grow up too quickly. "I'm not going to let Venus pass up her childhood. Long after tennis is over, I want her to know who she is."

The decision to take her out of the junior tournaments made Venus "the sport's great experiment," as one writer put it. "No player of the modern game, male or female, has achieved stature without testing and refining his or her game in juniors."

Soon enough, the results of the experiment would be in.

3

HOW YOUNG
IS TOO YOUNG?

❧

DESPITE RICHARD WILLIAMS' athletic
abilities, his daughter Venus soon outmatched him
by a wide margin on the tennis court. In 1991,
when Venus was almost 11 and a half years old, the
family moved to Florida so that Venus could start
training with coach Richard Macci at his international tennis academy, near Orlando. She was by
this time the top-ranked 12-and-under player in
southern California, and was unbeaten in 63
matches before pulling out of the junior circuit.

Earlier that year, at Richard Williams' invita-
tion the renowned Rick Macci had come all the
way to Compton to watch Venus and Serena strut
their stuff on the glass-strewn "East Compton Hills
Country Club." While homeless people and drug
addicts lay passed out on the grass nearby, Macci
hit balls with the sisters and found himself in awe
of their tennis talent and athleticism in general.
Within an hour, he later said, he was sure Venus
could be a world-class player. As if her prowess
with the racquet wasn't enough to impress the
world-famous coach, Venus later showed off by
walking on her hands and doing back-flips. "I
believed both Venus and Serena had champion
written all over them," Macci said. "I had no doubt
that Venus could be prime time."

Macci's famous academy was expensive: up to

*Venus, age 12, is shown here
practicing a two-handed backhand
shot. Venus started playing tennis
when she was only four years old.*

40 young players paid $2,200 per month for room, board, tennis instruction, and transportation back and forth from school. Macci had previously offered scholarships to needy students, such as Jennifer Capriati and Mary Pierce. Now Venus and Serena would be brought into the fold—they'd leave the ghetto and enter one of the sport's elite training centers. Venus and Serena received full scholarships, and the whole family received free housing. "I wouldn't have made the commitment to the family if I didn't think [Venus] could be No. 1 in the world," Macci later explained. "Our agreement was if the girls were successful, that's when the financial arrangement would kick in."

In Florida, Venus spent six hours a day, six days a week training with Coach Macci—a grueling schedule she adhered to for four years. She was quickly approaching her full adult height and weight of 6' 1" and 155 pounds, and she was becoming incredibly fast and strong. But she was still an "experiment"—she had stuck to her family's decision to stay out of junior competition.

Although they were now far from their community roots in Compton, the Williamses were still very deeply bonded to one another. Years earlier Oracene had become a member of Jehovah's Witnesses, an evangelical Christian sect with rigorous rules on how followers should live their lives. Although Richard did not join the group himself, he encouraged his wife to raise all their daughters in the faith. In Florida, Oracene and all the girls attended worship services three times a week and preached door-to-door as required by their faith (a practice they continued even when Venus and Serena were world-famous and lived in a wealthy neighborhood). They also abided by the sect's stringent rules—for example, no birthday or Christmas celebrations were allowed.

Although Venus did attend a public middle school for the first year of her training with Macci, she eventually opted for homeschooling so as to better accommodate her tennis schedule. This also helped Oracene and Richard maintain control of how their kids were being raised. Devotion to their faith and the decision to homeschool may have isolated the girls from other children, but it kept the family very close-knit. In a sense, the Williams family's choices were always about doing things their own way, choosing their own paths, whether it came to religious discipline or athletic development.

But there had always been a paradox at the heart of the Williams family, at least from the perspective of the public. On the one hand, Richard had apparently done almost everything in his power to encourage Venus's abilities and feed her natural competitiveness and ambition—and would continue to do so. On the other hand, he often disassociated himself from Venus's success, at one point even claiming that he'd been trying to encourage her to quit tennis. These two somewhat contradictory attitudes would play out again and again in Richard's words and actions—or at least, in the way the press reported on his words and actions.

Regardless of his ambitions for his two tennis-playing daughters, it was clear that he was sincerely concerned for them. He spoke to reporters of his worries that they might get in too deep and too fast when it came to playing professionally. He'd spent a lot of time contemplating the careers of gifted young athletes who were crushed by the pressures of professional sports and looked for solace in drugs or other self-destructive behavior. He wasn't going to be a "fool" like Jennifer Capriati's dad, he once told an interviewer. Capriati had shot to the top of the ranks and then plummeted to the depths of marijuana addiction in the space of just a few years. "She was a great kid at fourteen. At fifteen, she lost her smile. At sixteen, there were problems. What happened? I want to make sure that doesn't happen to my kids," Richard said. He repeatedly insisted that he would never allow his daughters to turn pro at 14, and once even said—in typical Richard Williams, over-the-top fashion—that any parent who did so "should be shot."

But Venus was the proverbial apple that didn't fall far from the tree: she was the willful daughter of willful Richard, and by the time she was in her early teens, she was pushing hard to do things her own way. "I march to my own drummer," she would later say. Despite her parents' reservations and concerns—and after three years of training but no tournaments—Venus desperately wanted to begin competing again.

Richard and Oracene Williams were hardly alone in their fears about the kind of stress faced by young girls on the pro tour. In September 1994, the Women's Tennis Council (WTC)—the national organization that runs women's professional tennis in the country—announced that new age limits for participation in the women's pro tour would take effect as of January 1, 1995. Under the outgoing rules, girls as young as 14 were allowed to play in as many as 12 tour events and the season-ending Virginia Slims championship. But the Council had come to realize that teenagers on tour were risking serious medical and psychological problems. Under the new rules, 14-year-olds would be barred from tour events. At 15, they would be permitted to enter a limited number of events, with that number increasing each year until age 18, when they would be free to play a full schedule.

The WTC, however, made a controversial decision to include a "grandfather clause" in its new rules, meaning players who turned 14 before the end of the year—including Venus as well as Swiss rising star Martina Hingis—would not be barred from tour events. The WTC said it wouldn't be fair to these young players to change the ground rules just as they were about to embark on their careers,

Jennifer Capriati returned to the courts in 1996 after a long absence due to personal problems. Capriati served as an example to the Williamses of the potential problems of becoming a professional player at an early age.

but some cynical observers had a different take on the situation. One *Sports Illustrated* commentator suspected that the real motivation was a fear of lawsuits from parents, and even suggested that the WTC had worked together with Richard Williams on the new eligibility rules so as not to delay Venus's chance to turn pro.

During this period, Williams insisted that the decision to turn pro was all Venus's. He even told one reporter, rather unbelievably, "I've been trying to get her to quit [tennis] since she was eight." But the press had trouble believing that this take-charge father—the man who'd pulled Venus out of junior competition, despite all advice to the contrary—had no control over his daughter's career choices. They continued to needle him about it, even after Venus's stunning professional debut in late October 1994. "Richard says he is setting his own rules, but just how much has he defied the system?" asked one skeptical sports writer. "Venus is the product of a Florida tennis academy. She spends an average of four hours a day on court. She has left the conventional school system. She is a pro at 14, although her father insists he had nothing to do with that decision." In other words, how different was her life from that of a young, overworked Jennifer Capriati?

Veteran sports commentator Frank Deford seemed particularly incensed by WTC's decision to change the rules but still let in the current crop of adolescent players. He charged the Council with hypocrisy, comparing its actions with "the old vaudeville comedian holding up his left hand to modestly halt the applause for his jokes, while with his right hand he wiggles it to solicit more cheers." In an editorial on National Public Radio, a public radio station, Deford railed against what he called "puberty tennis" for teenage girls— even subtly implying that it was a form of child exploitation.

> Because girls' bodies mature earlier and earlier, but because their minds remain childishly incomplete, they fall easily under the thrall of those men their parents select to teach, rote, how to swing a two-handed backhand or how to walk the balance beam or how to perform a double salchow. So long, too, as we have these sprites to distract us, all women's sport will be stunted. Puberty exportation diverts interest from the top female grown-ups that we should be watching, just as we do, after all, watch the men play men's sports.

The debate about girls in professional tennis

would continue on through the years. Meanwhile, Venus ignored the controversy and followed through on her decision. At the Bank of the West Classic held in Oakland, California, the 14-year-old tennis "debutante" demolished the 59th-ranked player, Shaun Stafford, in about an hour of play in two straight sets, 6–3, 6–4. Although Venus didn't completely live up to her own pre-game hype (for example, she didn't fulfill her earlier promises to "serve big" and come into the net often), she did display a competent serve and strong ground strokes. Most importantly, according to one commentator, Venus demonstrated "command of herself." She proved that she was not "a fawn trapped in the headlights of an onrushing career," but a "bright, witty kid with a supportive family."

Richard Williams, cagey and inscrutable as ever, claimed not to be thrilled by his daughter's victory and had even spent part of the match rooting for Shaun to win. "I wish [Venus] had lost," he said afterwards. "I think junior players ought to struggle. When they start winning, it's just like a drunk who wants one more drink. When they win, kids want to play one more tournament. I wanted Shaun to win so I could say to Venus, 'I told you so.'"

Later that day, he even went up to Arantxa Sanchez-Vicario, the No. 2 player in the world and the tournament's top-seeded player, who would face Venus in the next round. Shaking her hand vigorously, he said, "I hope you win." Sanchez-Vicario eyed Williams with a mixture of suspicion and amusement. "You hope I win?" she asked.

For better or worse, Richard Williams got his wish. Venus played a thrilling match against Sanchez-Vicario, serving hard and hitting fast ground strokes, but ultimately lost. Still, Venus's efforts at her first pro tournament impressed a lot of people. Tennis veteran Pam Shriver said the

Venus Williams (center) and her father, Richard Williams (left), make an appearance on the Montel Williams Show *on September 25, 1997.*

girl still needed time to develop into a top player, but noted, "I think she has a lot of weapons." Coach Rick Macci agreed that Venus needed a lot more experience to become truly dominant on the court. Venus would soon get that experience, although at a pace closely monitored by her family: Richard would allow Venus to enter only a very limited number of events in the coming years. It was a workable compromise between a willful daughter and her willful father. And although

Rick Macci wanted to see his new star succeed, he appreciated the family approach of the Williams.

"You've got to give Richard a lot of credit. He wants her to take it slow, and that says a lot about him as a dad. You've got to respect him for that."

4

THE GO-SLOW PRO

‹•›

IN AUGUST 1995, Jack Kramer, a tennis legend who had observed and promoted the careers of many world-class women players over the decades, told *USA Today* that Venus Williams "just might be the greatest of them all." Like Richard Macci, John McEnroe, and so many others in the sport, Kramer had caught an early case of Venus fever. Venus and her father weren't shy about making such bold predictions themselves—Venus had been telling people she was going to be number one since she was six years old.

The clothing manufacturer Reebok had caught the bug as well. It believed Venus was going to be a superstar and had recently signed her to a multimillion-dollar endorsement contract. The company also hired Richard Williams as a paid consultant to its urban-youth outreach program, although for some unknown reason he chose to deny the arrangement in the press. Other companies came calling, but the Williams family declined their offers, saying their daughter was still too young to spend a lot of time endorsing racquets or other products for manufacturers hoping to benefit from Venus's fame. Nevertheless, Venus was already a huge success by one measure: she had pulled her entire family out of poverty with a few strokes of her contract-signing pen. The Williams moved to a lush 10-acre estate near West Palm Beach, Florida, where Venus and Serena

Venus reaches for a difficult shot. Her aggressive game style helped her gain recognition early in her tennis career.

had their own private tennis courts to practice on—with not a single drug needle, bullet casing, or broken glass bottle in sight.

On some level, it didn't matter whether Venus had proven herself on the courts yet. For years now, whenever she traveled to tennis events, she'd also make a point to run tennis clinics for poor inner-city kids who dared to dream big dreams despite the limitations of their environment. She was already a winner in their eyes. It was this aspect of her success that Richard Williams referred to when he made another of his over-the-top remarks to the press in 1995. "I don't know anyone who's done what Venus did," he said. "She should go right to the Hall of Fame. She's going to be there anyway, so why waste time?"

For more detached observers, however, Venus was still an unknown quantity. She had made her pro debut in October at the Bank of the West Classic, where she played with fortitude but ultimately lost to Arantxa Sanchez-Vicario of Spain, ranked No. 2. Now 15 years old, Venus had not played another professional event in almost a year. She would have to play another two tournaments before she even received a ranking from the Women's Tennis Association (WTA, formerly called the Women's Tennis Council). Until Venus started competing more often and proving herself, any predictions of her future greatness would be considered mere hype.

Richard had worked out a compromise with his daughter. He'd agreed to let her go pro at 14 against his wishes, but she'd have to proceed at a very controlled pace. She'd be allowed to play in only three tournaments in 1995, only six the following years, and no Grand Slam events (Wimbledon and the Australian, French, and U.S. Opens) until she was 17. She'd have to stay in school (a private school she'd recently entered) and maintain an A average all the way through. By strictly limiting her exposure to the pro circuit and keeping her focused on her educational priorities, Richard and Oracene hoped to protect their daughter from some of the more stressful aspects of the tennis business. Venus had come around to accept their way of thinking. Just before playing in the Acura Classic at the Manhattan Country Club in New York City, Venus told reporters, "Playing fewer tournaments has nothing to do with me thinking I can be the best. The reason I don't want to play in all these tournaments is because you stay in hotels for weeks and weeks, and I am too young for that."

A sports psychologist named Jim Loehr went on the record to say he endorsed Venus's go-slow approach. "A young player should be brought into the pro arena gradually. It's not just how they handle matches, but everything, the press, the losses, and just being away from a normal environment."

As it turned out, during the next few years Venus got a lot of practice in handling losses at professional events—maybe more than she would have hoped for. Her 1995 season came and went with only one noteworthy win, a thrilling upset against 18th-ranked Amy Frazier in the second round of the 1995 Bank of the West Classic. In 1996 she did win 7 of her 12 matches, but she earned no titles and didn't even make it to the final round of any event. To help keep her spirits up, Richard made a deal with Venus to pay her fifty dollars each time she lost. "Venus says she has more fifty-dollar bills than she knows what to do with," he said.

Her serves were being recorded at phenomenal speeds for a player so young—108 miles per hour and upwards—but she acknowledged she still had plenty of work to do on her game, particularly her volleys, her slice, and her attack on short balls. "I want more of an aggressive game," she told reporters. After several years of solid groundwork with Rick Macci, Venus was back to having her father as coach. She continued to excel at school and spoke frequently about her desire to go on to college. She was looking to the future, but clearly she had much yet to accomplish in tennis—

With her hair braided in the purple and green colors of the All England Club, Venus reaches for a forehand shot during a first-round match at Wimbledon in June 1997.

especially now that her younger sister, Serena, was quickly catching up to her big sister in speed, power, and skill.

In 1997, Venus Williams began the season ranked at a lackluster 211. Skeptics began to wonder whether Venus would ever live up to the hopes—and the hype—that had surrounded her since early childhood. But suddenly, Venus started proving the skeptics wrong. In March of that year, at the Evert Cup in Indian Wells, California, Venus beat her first top-10 player, upsetting the fifth-ranked Iva Majoli of Croatia. A particularly dramatic moment came in the 10th game of the third set. Majoli threatened to win during two match points against Venus's serve, but Venus took both points, the second one with an ace (a single, powerful serve that rushes past the opponent to win the point). A few days later in Florida, Venus defeated an unseeded player named Ginger Helgeson Nielson in the first round of the Lipton Championships—her first victory in her home state since she'd turned pro three years earlier. Venus kept her cool and played her best tennis despite a brief interruption—the appearance of a rat in the stands. The sight of the rodent had fans on their feet and screaming until tournament workers were finally able to capture it.

In late May Venus went to the French Open—her first event played on clay courts. Wearing a shining silver dress and bright white beads in her hair, she won a gripping match against the 41st-ranked player, Naoko Sawamatsu of Japan. Venus was eliminated in a later round of the French Open, but her first Grand Slam event helped prime her for the rest of the season. She continued to play tournaments throughout the summer and to pick up early-round wins—as well as substantial paychecks.

By July, when Wimbledon began, she was ranked 59th and had earned more than $50,000 in prize money. Wimbledon, the famous English Grand Slam event played on grass courts, was a disappointment for Venus. She started out strongly in her first-round match against Poland's Magdalena Grzybowska, serving at 114 miles an hour and playing her characteristically powerful game. But Grzybowska began ripping backhands deep and down the line, eventually wearing her opponent down. Early in the third set, Venus went lunging for a shot and ended up with her face planted in the grass court. She lost the match in three sets. One commentator said that Venus now "stood revealed as a huge talent with little idea of how to adjust to an opponent or adversity."

But the season wasn't over. Venus was taking her

licks, but at the U.S. Open in September, she demonstrated that she'd been learning from her losses. Venus began taking speed off her serve and her ground strokes, and started mixing up her shots to keep her opponent guessing. Her control improved and she began to complement her great power and speed with clear-cut strategy. Watching her daughter practice before the Open, Oracene noticed a remarkable improvement, and later told a reporter, "something in [Venus's] head finally clicked."

When the tournament began at the new Arthur Ashe stadium in Flushing Meadows, Queens, Venus played smarter than she had before and outwitted her opponents. She defeated higher-ranking players in four rounds of the event, and then in the final faced the number one women's player, her arch-rival and fellow tough-talking teen, Martina Hingis of Switzerland.

Earlier in the year, Hingis had already beaten Venus at the Toshiba Tennis Classic. At the Open, Venus put up a good fight but was defeated. Although Hingis walked away with the title, Venus had moved up in rank to a very respectable No. 27—a stunning improvement over her rank of 211 at the start of the year. A *Sports Illustrated* commentator confirmed the general consensus when he wrote, "Williams's progress as a player was undeniable; almost overnight she had become a force every player but one fears." Yet even that "one" who didn't fear her—Hingis—was willing to acknowledge Venus's vast improvement. "She got better and better," Hingis said after the U.S. Open final. "For the first time she showed that she can play great."

In a special way, the 1997 U.S. Open had been the perfect event for Venus to begin proving herself and living up to the title of "Cinderella of the ghetto," as her father called her. The event that year celebrated two black tennis greats. It began on Althea Gibson's 70th birthday, and the opening

Venus and Martina Hingis of Switzerland celebrate Hingis's victory at the U.S. Open championship match in September 1997.

ceremonies featured a tribute to sports legend Arthur Ashe, whose widow was on hand to give a speech about "inclusion" in the sport of tennis.

A reporter asked Venus whether she might become the sports world's next Tiger Woods—the young golf prodigy who once described his ethnic background as "Cablasian," to acknowledge his mixed Caucasian, Black, and Asian roots, and who had forever changed the lily-white image of professional golf.

"I would hope so," Venus said, with typical brio. "He's different from the mainstream, and in tennis I also am. I'm tall. I'm black. Everything's different about me. Just face the facts."

5

ON THE SHOULDERS
OF GIANTS

VENUS WILLIAMS FIRST endured snobbish, racist comments at the exclusive country clubs where she and her sister competed as children. Such comments were in a way an echo of tennis's long, elitist history. The sport of tennis was originally developed in France in the 15th century, where aristocratic ladies and gentlemen played the game. By the mid-19th century, the game had spread across Europe and to the United States and become a competitive sport for the best men players and a smaller percentage of women (who would win trinkets such as silver mirrors and hairbrushes, rather than prize money).

The spectators at a growing number of championship events were still exclusively white upper-class men and women. In 1916, just before World War I, black tennis players formed their own national organization, but the United States Lawn Tennis Association (USLTA)—as well as the private clubs that hosted USLTA events—continued to bar all nonwhites until the late 1940s. In the period after World War II, as the country responded to the growing civil rights movement, the women's movement, and other broad social and economic changes, things started to change in the closed, clubby world of tennis.

Still, black players, whether men or women, remained very rare. But decades before Venus and Serena shot up the ranks of the women's game and

Althea Gibson shows her fierce competitive nature during a title match with Darlene Hard at Wimbledon in 1957. Gibson was the first black athlete to win the tournament.

became international celebrities, there were two great black tennis players in particular who helped pave the path for the Williams sisters: Althea Gibson and Arthur Ashe Jr. Just as young Venus and Serena were "unlikely" tennis players on account of their background, neither Gibson nor Ashe seemed destined to become sports legends when they were children—Gibson because she was a troublemaker from a troubled home; Ashe because he was thin and unhealthy as a child.

Althea Gibson was born in South Carolina in 1927 and spent her first few years on a tiny five-acre farm. During the Great Depression, as jobs became scarce and life on the farm got particularly tough, her parents decided to send Althea to live in New York City with her mother's sister. It was hardly a healthy environment for a child: Aunt Sally lived in Harlem and made her living as a bootlegger, selling home-made liquor out of her apartment. (The Prohibition Act of 1919 was intended to abolish alcohol use by making it illegal, but instead had spawned a nation-wide network of black-market businesses.) Although Althea's parents eventually came to New York and moved in with Aunt Sally, their young daughter spent a lot of time unsupervised. She grew rebellious and wild—stealing, getting into fights with boys, playing hooky from school, and generally disrespecting and disobeying her parents.

Soon, Althea found athletic outlets for her wild-ness and hyperactivity. She fell in love with basketball and baseball, which she often played with other tough, truant, neighborhood kids right in the middle of the busy city streets. At 5' 10", 140 pounds, Althea was a fierce competitor even among the neighborhood boys. In the summers, the Police Athletic League would sometimes create makeshift "playgrounds" by roping off some of the streets to allow children to play safely.

In 1941, Gibson was at one of these playgrounds playing paddleball (a slower version of tennis, played with a paddle instead of a racquet) when a wealthy Harlem bandleader named Buddy Walker noticed her. Impressed by her strength, her aggressiveness, and the speed of her shots, Walker invited her to learn tennis at the Harlem River Tennis Courts, a club for wealthy blacks. Decades later, Buddy Walker was certainly one of the people Althea referred to when she said, "If I made it, it's half because I was game enough to take a lot of punishment along the way and half because there were a lot of people who cared enough to help me."

Given a helpful push by Walker, Althea devoted herself to learning and excelling at the game, and soon began dominating the tournaments offered by the American Tennis Association (an all-black counterpart to the mainstream tennis organizations, which were still segregated). Eventually, a wealthy South Carolina businessman took Althea under his wing during her high school years, paying for her private tennis lessons. She later finished her college degree at Florida A&M University.

From 1947 to 1956, Gibson won 10 consecutive ATA women's singles tournaments. In 1950, the Orange Lawn Tennis Club in South Orange, New Jersey, broke with its segregated tradition and invited Althea to play in its national grass court championship, where she won her first match but lost to Louise Brough in the second round. Soon, other previously all-white tennis associations began to open their events to this competitive newcomer. Althea played well in many tournaments throughout the 1950s, but when she realized she wasn't winning any major titles, she began to contemplate retirement. Still, she stuck with it, and in 1957, on a 100-degree afternoon, she played two superlative sets against Darlene Hard to win Wimbledon. "At last, at last," an exhausted Althea said as the match ended. She was the first black athlete to win the event.

Althea Gibson proudly showcases her trophies for winning the national women's singles championship in 1957 at the West Side Tennis Club in Forest Hills, New York. Gibson won the title again in 1958; a black woman would not take another Grand Slam title until Serena Williams won at Wimbledon in 1999.

After this historic triumph, New York City honored Althea with a ticker-tape parade. Soon after, she won the U.S. Open at Forest Hills, and then held on to both her majors titles for another year in 1958. She retired from amateur tennis shortly thereafter, and went on to record an album of her singing, appear in a film, and play professional golf for a few years in the 1960s. She eventually withdrew from competitive athletics altogether after suffering several illnesses. In 1975 she began working as the manager of the East Orange, New Jersey, recreation department. Although no longer actively involved in sports and living a quiet life in New Jersey, Althea Gibson is still a guiding and inspiring presence for young African-American athletes everywhere.

In sharp contrast to young Althea, the wild child, Arthur Ashe Jr. was an impeccably well-mannered and studious young man from a loving but strictly run household. Born in 1943 in Richmond, Virginia, Ashe was the son of a police officer who'd been put in charge of the Brook Field, a sprawling 18-acre, blacks-only playground in this segregated city. Arthur Ashe Sr., his wife, and two sons lived in a five-room frame house in the middle of the park, surrounded by tennis courts, basketball courts, baseball diamonds, and an Olympic-sized pool. Arthur Jr. was a skinny little child, not your typical young muscle-bound jock, and had suffered through measles, mumps, chicken pox, and other illnesses throughout child-hood—but he soon discovered he had extra-quick reflexes and an ability to think strategically. When he wasn't on the courts, young Arthur kept busy as an A student, a voracious reader, and an obedient son responsible for lots of chores.

Ashe's beloved mother died of complications during her third pregnancy when he was only six years old, a trauma that devastated Arthur's father and probably contributed to Arthur's own emotion-ally reserved demeanor as an adult. Despite the tragedy, Arthur continued to devote time to his studies and to hitting tennis balls off a backboard. When Arthur was seven, a university student and part-time tennis instructor named Ronald Charity offered to teach him, ultimately spending many hours correcting the young boy's strokes. Young Ashe began competing at tournaments in other all-black parks around Richmond, and found he enjoyed himself even when he wasn't winning.

When Arthur was 10, Ron Charity introduced him to Dr. Robert Walker Johnson, a successful doctor and avid tennis player in Lynchburg, Virginia, who had coached Althea Gibson and had won seven mixed doubles titles with her at the ATA national championships. Now retired from competition, Johnson had made it his mission to support young black tennis players by setting up a kind of summer camp for promising players in his home. Under Dr. Johnson's tutelage, Arthur deepened his knowledge of the game through drilling and exhaustive study about tennis strategy.

Ashe quickly rose through the ranks of the junior tournaments, all the while getting stellar grades in school. But there was one major barrier to his improvement: no indoor winter courts in Richmond were available to blacks. If he wanted to become a serious competitor, he needed to play year-round—which meant leaving the segregated South. He moved to St. Louis and learned a more aggressive playing style from a club pro there named Larry Miller.

Having graduated top of his high school class, Arthur Ashe Jr. was recruited and offered a scholarship to play on the UCLA men's tennis team. After college (where he majored in business), he continued playing and quickly moved up the amateur ranks. In 1963, as a 20-year-old, he became the first African American on the U.S. Davis Cup team, and eventually won 28 out of 34 Cup matches over the next 15 years.

As of 1968, tennis tournaments began to carry significant prize money for players who devoted themselves to a professional tennis career. Tennis was considered to be "open" to anyone who could learn the game and excel at it—not just the people rich enough to belong to exclusive private clubs—and not just whites.

In 1968, Ashe became the first U.S. Open champion in the open era. He turned professional in 1970, won the Australian Open, and then, two years later, became the first American tennis player to exceed $100,000 in annual earnings. Ashe had a

huge triumph against the game's number one male player, Jimmy Connors, in the 1975 Wimbledon finals. A magazine editor at the time wrote, "Seeing a black man playing tennis was weird in itself, but seeing him win the most prestigious tournament in the world by himself in a manner that belied everything Americans seemed to hold true about black Americans was something that was pretty indescribable."

Arthur Ashe's tennis career was cut short by a heart attack in 1979. But during his retirement, Ashe became a kind of elder statesman and activist

Arthur Ashe lunges at a return from Jimmy Connors in the 1975 Wimbledon finals, which Ashe won. He was the first African American to play with the U.S. Davis Cup team and was the team captain later in his career.

for many causes and issues, especially ones having to do with race. He formed athletic associations for African Americans, wrote a three-volume history of blacks in sports, and devoted much of his efforts to the American Heart Association, the United Negro College Fund, and a U.S. foreign policy think tank called TransAfrica.

His years of top-notch athleticism had not, unfortunately, erased the destiny his sickly childhood seemed to forge for him. Following his heart attack and quadruple bypass surgery in 1979, Ashe required another operation in 1983. During the blood transfusion, he acquired HIV. (This was in the years before hospitals were required to test donated blood for the virus that causes AIDS.) Although Ashe hid the diagnosis from the public for a while, he was eventually forced into the limelight by the press, soon after basketball hero Magic Johnson had made his own announcement about having HIV. Reluctant at first to become a spokesperson for the disease, Ashe eventually started a foundation for the defeat of AIDS and lobbied the United Nations for more AIDS research funding worldwide. Ashe died in 1993.

In 1996, his hometown of Richmond, the city that once forbade him to play tennis with white children and that kept him out of indoor, year-round courts while he was trying to improve his game, erected a memorial statue of him on Monument Avenue.

Since the late 1960s tennis had grown in popularity as it became a more inclusive game, open to male and female players of all ages, races, and nationalities, played in large public stadiums, and broadcast to the televisions of many millions of viewers. But for the most part it had still remained a primarily upper-middle-class endeavor, one that required the kind of leisure time and access to training that very poor children usually don't have. Venus and Serena Williams were considered outsiders, having come from the poor neighborhood of Compton.

6

OUTSIDER AND INSIDER

———— ❧ ————

WHAT KIND OF person is Venus Williams? Answering that question ought to be fairly easy—after all, Venus has been a national celebrity since she was in the fifth grade. The story of her life has been told again and again in the press, and continues to be told in newspapers, books, magazines, and television programs. So it's natural that many of her fans and supporters would feel they know Venus well.

Many consider her to be a young woman with a brash personality and a tendency to boast. She has a bold, colorful, and up-to-the-second fashionable taste in clothing and enjoys loud, guitar-based music, preferably alternative rock groups like Nirvana, Hole, and Green Day. She did very well in high school, graduating with a 3.8 GPA, and loved subjects like history and paleontology (the study of fossils and prehistoric life forms). Fans know that she is extremely close to her family, particularly her kid sister and fellow tennis champ, Serena.

The thing about being a celebrity, however, is that all the repeated storytelling and image-making tend to reduce the person to a one-dimensional, simplified version of herself or himself. In reality, the people we admire and worship as living legends —sports stars, musicians, writers, Hollywood

Venus Williams celebrates her defeat of South Africa's Joannette Kruger at the U.S. Open in August 1997.

actors—are just as complicated (and sometimes contradictory) as people who are not in the spotlight. Many of their star qualities are admirable, but they have flaws and rough edges like everyone else. Arguably, this makes celebrities more interesting, not less.

The 1997 U.S. Open was a real turning point in Venus's tennis career. Even though she lost the finals to fellow teen star Martina Hingis, Venus demonstrated that she had the potential to be number one. But behind the battles that took place on the tennis court, there were other kinds of rivalries brewing and interpersonal wars being waged. Part of the problem stemmed from the fact that Venus and her family deliberately stayed aloof from other tennis players. In keeping with her religious faith and her strong devotion to her family, Venus didn't make it a priority to befriend other tennis players or make small talk with them in the locker rooms. "We couldn't care less what people think of us" was how Richard Williams summed up their attitude.

Keeping to herself was a choice Venus had every right to make, and in some ways, it was quite admirable: Venus wasn't going to waste time "making nice" with people just because it was considered the proper thing to do. She had always been generous and charming when it came to interacting with her fans, particularly those crowds of young black girls sporting beaded braids and obviously worshipping Venus as a role model. But as an outsider in the mostly white, predominantly upper-class world of tennis, she was not interested in pretending to be an insider.

"I'm looking to win matches, to be the best. I'm not looking for friends," Venus said. "You can't really find a friend these days. You have your family, you have your God, and that's about it."

Admirable as it might have been from one per-

spective, Venus's independence and aloofness rubbed some people the wrong way, and helped turn the usual amicable rivalries between competing players into bitter personal conflicts. Some of these conflicts had unfortunate racial overtones. Just before the on-court Williams versus Hingis showdown, other players on the tour complained publicly about what they considered to be Venus's arrogance, unfriendliness, and out-of-control boasting. A sportswriter noted at the time that Hingis was also infamous for saying cocky things, but got away with it because she did it with a pleasant grin and was always friendly to fellow players.

In response to the public complaints, Oracene Williams expressed concerns about racism on the tour. Soon afterwards, Venus's semifinals competitor, the 11th-seeded Irina Spirlea, intentionally

Serena (center), Venus (right), and their mother, Oracene Williams, leave the practice court at the 1998 Australian Open Tennis Championships several hours before the two are scheduled to play each other. Venus went on to win the second-round match over Serena.

collided with Venus during the changeover (when players switch sides on the court). Spirlea later told reporters she did it because of Venus's arrogance, but Richard Williams attributed it to racism and told the press that he and Venus had heard the racial epithet "nigger" used against them by other players. He then went on to call Spirlea "a big, ugly, tall, white turkey"—a comment that offended many white people, even those who sympathized with the Williams family.

These incidents and counter-incidents distracted everyone from the tennis itself. *Sports Illustrated* reported that just after Venus lost to Hingis in the final, her press conference deteriorated as white reporters tried to browbeat her into discussing her father's inflammatory remarks.

As words flew, Venus seemed to shrink in her chair. "I think with this moment in the first year in Arthur Ashe Stadium, it all represents everyone being together, everyone having a chance to play," she said. "So I think this is definitely ruining the mood, these questions about racism."

It was a coy response in some ways—after all, it had been Venus's mother who'd broached the issue of racism in the first place and Venus's father who'd fanned the flames (whether intentionally or not) with his own comments. But it also revealed Venus's frustration at being caught in a tough situation.

Venus, just like her father, has always been open about her humble roots in Compton and her close ties to the black community in which she grew up. She has taken on the role of "ghetto Cinderella" with enthusiasm and has gladly become an inspiration for inner-city children hoping to develop their talents and succeed like her. She has never tried to be somebody she isn't, has never pretended to fit in perfectly with the elite tennis establishment. A generation earlier, even a great tennis hero such as Arthur Ashe found it necessary to maintain his easy-going, dignified, non-provocative demeanor just to defuse the potential for racial tensions on tour. But decades later, in what seems to be a more enlightened world, a very proud black girl like Venus is not interested in assimilating or toning down the rough edges of her personality just to avoid conflict.

Besides, any unfriendliness Venus exhibits toward other players in the locker room or on the court is counterbalanced by the charm and enthusiasm with which she meets the press and her fans. Tennis-lovers must be intrigued by any 17-year-old who could confidently tell reporters she could one day "save" U.S. tennis, just moments before losing at Wimbledon in 1997. A clear example of this fascination is evident in sportswriter S. L. Price's description of Venus's showing at the 1997 U.S. Open. "Williams sailed into the Open's second week, shaking her beaded braids, seducing the camera with her quirky exuberance," Price wrote.

For better or worse, Price went on to say, tennis's popularity with fans has always depended on the personality of its players:

> Such dependence on personality has been tennis's curse and blessing since the open era began, and nothing will change that. The sport's eternal good news, of course, is that with all the mourning about the old days, it takes only a few compelling new faces to bring the excitement back. The bad news is that when personalities dry up, tennis does too—no matter how well it's being played.

Price also suggested that Venus is a badly needed female counterpart to Andre Agassi, the extremely charismatic and talented player who helped renew interest in the sport and who "got a legion of balding white men to shave their heads and grow bad

Venus Williams hands out beads to the crowd after her victory over France's Sandrine Testude at the 1997 U.S. Open.

goatees." Venus may not be number one yet, and in fact she may never get there—but by the grace of her complex and colorful personality, she may end up "saving" women's tennis, anyway.

So what kind of person is Venus Williams? A person who is friendly in some situations and not so friendly in others—just like most human beings. A person with some conflicts and issues about race—like most human beings. But also, a person whose contradictory nature and willingness to say what's on her mind makes her tremendously appealing to watch and listen to. If she were always sweet and kind and amiable, if there weren't a little vinegar mixed into her personality, she wouldn't fascinate us so much.

7

PRIME TIME FOR WOMEN

—— ❧ ——

Venus and Serena Williams face each other at the 1999 Lipton Championship in Key Biscayne, Florida. In February of that year, Venus and Serena became the first sister duo to win singles titles on the WTA tour on the same day.

WOMEN'S TENNIS, ONCE considered relatively boring, grew phenomenally as a spectator sport during the mid-1990s. Although the predominance of adolescent girls in women's tennis had caused some critics to complain and some concerned observers to question whether these girls were being pushed into the pro arena too quickly, the presence of teen stars had everything to do with the sports' surge in popularity. There was the charmingly haughty Martina Hingis, with her intuitive ability to anticipate her opponent's moves and her dead-on placement of returns and drop shots—skills that helped her dominate physically stronger players and that enabled her to become at 16 the youngest person ever to achieve a number one ranking. There was the beautiful and glamorous Anna Kournikova, a native of Moscow who was spotted practicing at age 10 by a sports agent and whisked away to a Florida tennis academy, and who was ranked at No. 11 in the early part of 1998. And there were the Williams sisters—tall, strong, brassy, and ultra-confident.

"Is it mere coincidence that such an exciting crop of teenagers has come together at the same time?" asked the British magazine *The Economist*. "Perhaps not. For talented female athletes today, tennis is the most lucrative sporting choice, and all [these] teenage contenders come from less than privileged backgrounds."

The magazine went further to suggest that the new WTA rules—by which female players were limited to a certain number of professional events between their 15th and 18th birthdays—had contributed to the success of these "teeny smashers" who were revamping women's tennis: "As a result [of the WTA age restrictions], the new teen sensations have had time to develop a more rounded game than their metronomic base-line predecessors." (In other words, the newer teen players were playing more strategically and aggressively.) "At the same time, new racket technology has added zest to the women's game. The emphasis on power which has taken so much of the finesse out of men's play has helped make women's matches faster, less predictable and more entertaining."

Another magazine, *Time International*, noted similarly that "[a]lthough the men still command greater riches in prize money and sponsorships, they suffer from a perceived lack of personalities and a revolution in racket technology that can sometimes reduce the game to a stultifying exchange of booming serves."

After decades of taking a back seat to the more established men's game, women's tennis had begun to exceed it in terms of television ratings and overall popularity. Attendance at WTA tournaments rose from 2.4 million spectators in 1986 to 3.5 million in 1997—an increase of 45 percent—while the worldwide TV audience was estimated at 5.5 billion. Accordingly, more sports organizers were calling for equality in prize money for Grand Slam events. The U.S. Open had recently begun giving equal prizes to men and women competitors, but other events still lagged behind. Nevertheless, women's tennis had come a long, long way from the mid-19th century, when competitors played in ground-length skirts, corsets, and high collars, and could expect to receive pretty trinkets but no real money for their athletic "hobby." In the past 30 years, total annual prize money for all

The fashion styles of women's tennis players in the 1920s, as seen in this picture, greatly differed from those of today. The tournament prizes and other financial incentives were also substantially less.

women's professional events combined went from a laughable $250,000 to a whopping $40 million—and that doesn't even include the many millions in hefty endorsement fees earned by top players.

Venus Williams has been both a prime catalyst and a beneficiary of the sport's fantastic growth. She ended her smashing 1997 season at a very respectable ranking of No. 27 worldwide. Around this time, Venus told *Cosmopolitan* magazine that it was important for young women—even ambitious, confident ones—to set realistic goals for themselves. "For example, if I had said I wanted to be the number one tennis player in the world by the end of the year, I would have had to win every match I played. So this year [1997] my goal was to be in the top 20, a goal I thought I could reasonably achieve. Now, my goal for next year is to be number one."

As it turned out, Venus wouldn't quite achieve her own deadlines, but she did come awfully close. In January 1998 at the Australian Open, Venus came out in the first round to avenge her straight-set defeat to Martina Hingis the previous September, beating the Swiss superstar despite cramps in her right leg during the second set. She advanced to the second round to face her 16-year-old sister Serena (who'd turned pro one year after Venus did). Asked to compare the sisters' different approaches to tennis, their mother Oracene said, "Serena is a little meaner than Venus. I remind Serena about technical things and Venus about the mental side. I don't know who will win. But I do know when it is over, they will leave it on the court." It was their first match against each other as professionals—they hadn't opposed each other since a junior match eight years earlier, when Venus had trounced Serena. It was also the very first time in history that African-American sisters competed against each other in a pro event.

The match began with the two girls fairly evenly balanced, but then Venus began using her greater strength and her ability to stay calm to defeat her sibling, 7–6, 6–1, in 87 minutes. After the match, the Williams girls hugged each other and then bowed to the spectators together, hand in hand. The crowd responded with thunderous clapping and cheering. "It wasn't fun eliminating my little sister, but I have to be tough," Venus told reporters, who had overheard her apologizing to Serena with the words "I'm sorry I had to take you out." Serena responded lovingly, "If I had to lose . . . there's no one better to lose to than Venus."

(In any case, Serena's disappointment at losing

was nicely counteracted by some good news she received around that time: She finalized a deal with shoe manufacturer Puma, owned by the Hollywood-based entertainment group Regency Enterprises. The secret contract reportedly included an agreement by Regency to present Serena with potential opportunities in the fields of music, television, and movies. Whether in the world of tennis or somewhere beyond, both sisters were clearly planning on remaining stars for a long, long time to come.)

After those two thrilling games against Hingis and her own sister, Venus lost the Australian quarterfinals match to No. 2-ranked Lindsay Davenport. But just a few months later she won her first two professional singles titles—the first in March at the IGA Tennis Classic in Oklahoma City, where she demolished South Africa's Joannette Kruger 6–3, 6–2 in the finals and took home the $27,000 prize; and the second at the Lipton Championships in Key Biscayne. At the Lipton Venus got another shot at number one player Hingis during the semifinals—and prevailed again, clocking in record-breaking serves of 122 miles per hour despite continued trouble with her right leg and knee. In the finals Venus faced Anna Kournikova, who started out strongly but made a lot of unforced errors and eventually fell to her opponent's superior power game. Venus took home the $235,000 prize from that event. And in a move that boldly contradicted critics who called her unfriendly, Venus held her trophy aloft and waved to Kournikova, inviting her to join in the victory photographs.

After these two major victories, Venus's ranking jumped to No. 12 worldwide. She was excited to be within reasonable shot of the top ten, but she still managed to exude a solid sense of perspective. She spoke directly and honestly about her victory over her longtime rival, Hingis: "She isn't as strong as I am. A lot of times the strong person doesn't have to think as much as the next person. When I learn to

Venus (far left) and Serena Williams have both faced young stars Anna Kournikova (second to right) and Martina Hingis (far right) in singles competition. In 1999 Venus and Serena teamed up to win the French Open women's doubles title over Kournikova and Hingis.

[think more], I'm going to become a much better player." After all those years of bragging about her abilities and vowing to be number one, and after surviving the rancor and bitterness of the conflicts during the 1997 U.S. Open, Venus started to look at a much bigger picture. "Whether I am here playing tennis or not," she said, "tennis is going to go on with other people, so it's most important that I'm happy, that I'm enjoying myself whoever is playing."

The rest of the 1998 season went well for Venus. Although she did not make it past the quarterfinals at the French Open and Wimbledon—where she suffered a particularly tough defeat against the eventual winner, 29-year-old "veteran" Jana Novotna—she continued to improve her game, and managed to increase the speed of her already phenomenal serve. In June at Wimbledon, her serve was recorded at blistering 125 miles per hour, beating the previous record for all women by 2 miles per hour. As if that wasn't already a history-maker, Venus bested herself at the Swisscom Challenge with a serve of 127 miles per hour. She made it to the semifinals of the U.S. Open, but lost to the eventual champ Lindsay Davenport. Still, it had been a banner year—only two of her ten losses had been to players ranked below the top five. She was not number one yet, but she was certainly a viable contender.

Meanwhile, the presence of Venus, Serena, Anna, and Martina—all still teenagers, all so entrancing to their live spectators and TV audiences—had ensured another banner year for women's tennis overall. Paradoxically, the enthusiasm for these young players was helping regenerate interest in their older counterparts. Jana Novotna's stunning victories over Venus and Martina at Wimbledon were a prime example. A *Time* magazine writer offered this provocative assessment of the scene:

> For all their pizzazz and prowess, the four [Venus, Serena, Anna, and Martina] are hardly providing the real action on the tennis court. Instead, they have lit a fire under the tour's veteran players, who for a time last year seemed in danger of being edged out of the game. Emboldened by the bratty antics of their juniors, the "old ladies"—in tennis speak that's ages 22 to 35—are roaring back. And the generational battles have made for what Billie Jean King calls the "the greatest time in the history of women's tennis."

Hingis had dominated the field in 1997 and had become the youngest woman to win Wimbledon since 1887. But by September 1998, the tour veterans were pushing back hard. Arantxa Sanchez-Vicario, 26, and Monica Seles, 24, were the finalists at the French Open, while Jana Novotna, 29, and Nathalie Tauziat, 30, were the finalists at Wimbledon in July. These four got to the top by defeating their younger counterparts. In the fourth round of the French Open, Venus Williams got so frustrated at her trouncing by Sanchez-Vicario that she slammed a ball over the net and right in the direction of her opponent's head. Venus later threw a tantrum over a line call. To the press, Sanchez-Vicario quietly pointed to this kind of behavior as evidence of the younger player's immaturity. "I was very, very surprised that when she had an open court she was just trying to hit me—you know? That sometimes shows the personality on and off the court." Speaking about her own age group, the French Open champion added defiantly, "We were here before, and we're still here."

Even more than the Hingis-Williams rivalry of the previous year, the 1998 showdowns between older and younger female tennis players promised to keep fans emotionally involved in the happenings both on and off the court. As one commentator put it, "It's great tennis, but also it's great theater." Sportswriters noted that the older generation of players had been coasting along on stale strategies and familiar skills, but faced with the challenge from fresh, young, sassy players like Venus and Martina, they had begun to refine and improve their own games.

Twenty-two year old Lindsay Davenport, for example, had lost 25 pounds and grown considerably fitter. As a result, she had taken three tournaments in a row in the summer and was playing the best tennis of her career. The on-court generational rivalry had "inspired the older players—and I'll include myself in that group—to practice harder, to maybe want it more," Davenport said. "There's more of a sense that we don't want that 16-year-old to win a Grand Slam. It's given new life to the game."

Some of the older players disparaged the younger set for their bad on-court manners, their willingness to scream or curse at umpires and argue bad calls—tendencies that even Venus occasionally indulged in when she was frustrated. Still, some of that sassy attitude—reminiscent of John McEnroe's bad-boy days—was beginning to rub off on the older players as well. As one writer noted, during a match between the Czech Republic's Jana Novotna and Spain's Arantxa Sanchez-Vicario, "Novotna seemed veritably Venusized. During the heated second set, which went to a tiebreaker, the usually elegant Czech flipped the umpire the bird."

If nothing else, it was proof that Venus Williams and her cohort of sassy young players—in their athleticism and their personalities—had surely left a mark on the game of tennis.

8

SISTER, SISTER

ᘐ

DEPENDING ON WHICH day of the tennis season you catch them, they may be opponents, practice partners, or teammates for a doubles match. Sometimes they travel together to WTA events and cheer each other on from the stands, sometimes they're on different continents and have to keep in touch by E-mail. As with most siblings, their relationship has elements of competition and rivalry as well as cooperation and love. But one thing is clear: throughout it all, no matter who's winning or losing at tennis that day, Venus and Serena have remained best friends.

To the world, they are the tall, strong, phenomenal Williams sisters who knock down racial and economic barriers with each powerful ground stroke, each winning point. But to each other, they are simply "V" and "Mica" (MEE-kah)—their girlhood nicknames for one another. As professionals, they have no choice but to spend long hours each day practicing with each other. But after tennis, they go on and do the things that any other pair of close sisters might do. They study for their community college classes (Venus focuses on fashion design; Serena studies Spanish and psychology), shop at the mall, get manicures, surf and skateboard, braid and bead each other's hair (which takes many hours and thousands of beads to complete), listen to CDs, and dish about the cuties in the men's pro tennis line-up—Pete Sampras at the top of the list.

Serena (left) and Venus (right) display their fashion dolls. Each sister fantasizes about a second career in fashion design or some other creative, high-energy business.

They love tennis, but aren't fanatical about it. They talk about their eventual retirements from the sport with great ease and enthusiasm, because they're already busy planning and educating themselves for new challenges ahead. They are proudly independent about money, handling all their own accounts and paying their own taxes. "I just had to file my taxes," Venus once said. "I had to use all my hotel and plane ticket receipts I had saved. I think I've gotten over the pain of paying taxes. It's the price you have to pay for living in this country. I have to be able to do things for myself. . . . It feels good."

Both girls love to learn new languages, and always try to speak a little bit of the native tongue whenever they travel to international tournaments. (After winning a prize in Paris, Serena charmed her spectators by addressing them in textbook-perfect French.) As devout Jehovah's Witnesses, they attend church services several times a week and visit their neighbors door-to-door to inform them about the religion and, they hope, win a few converts. (It's a hard task when most people they meet would rather talk about tennis than religion, but the girls give it their best shot.) They involve themselves in charitable and civic causes—for example, by filming TV ads promoting seatbelt usage—and they fantasize about their second careers in fashion design or some other creative, high-energy business.

Venus and Serena Williams are barely out of their adolescence, they've got long lives ahead of them, so who knows what achievements they'll ultimately be remembered for? Yet even if the sisters were to drop out of the public view tomorrow—if they were to decide, suddenly, that they were tired of the limelight, had more money than they could possibly ever need, and simply wanted to stay home with their families, read good books, and pursue their various hobbies without international press coverage—they would still be remembered by their record-breaking, barrier-breaking appearances on the tennis court.

*Serena Williams prepares
to serve to Asa Carlsson of
Sweden in the first round of
the Gaz de France in 1999.
Serena won this match and the
tournament, taking home her
first professional singles title.*

In 1999, the standard 11-month tennis season began with some exciting intergenerational "warfare," courtesy of the Williams sisters, who each had a chance against 29-year-old German superstar Steffi Graf. Still a sentimental favorite among tennis fans, Graf was a 21-time Grand Slam winner and was once ranked at number one for a record 377 weeks. A decade earlier, she had revolutionized the women's game of tennis with her powerful forehands and serve—but this was before the world had seen what Venus and Serena could do.

At the Adidas International Tennis Tournament in Australia, Graf defeated Serena in a challenging three sets. After the match, Graf admitted that Serena threw her off her guard with some particularly powerful points. The next day in the quarterfinal rounds, Graf would face similar challenges from Venus. Serena suggested to a reporter that her older sister would be playing particularly hard—she'd be out for revenge on behalf of Serena's defeat. Nevertheless, Graf managed to fight off Venus's strong serves and aggressive playing style. Always a mentally tough player, Graf gutted it out and won the final four games of the last set, enabling her to take the match.

The Williams were swept out of this particular tournament, but it was a temporary setback. A few days after the Adidas tournament, both Serena and Venus were chosen—along with Seles and Davenport— to represent the United States in the 1999 Fed Cup Tennis Tournament, the premier women's international team tennis competition. There would be similar honors to come for both players. The year 1999, it turned out, would give both Serena and Venus plenty of opportunity to prevail over the game's toughest competitors—including each other!

In February, Venus and Serena made history as the first sister duo to win singles titles on the WTA tour on the same day. It was an unusual situation for the Williams sisters, who usually traveled together to events with one or both of their parents. But Serena, who turned pro the year after Venus, had recently started to emerge from her big sister's considerable shadow. Some observers even wondered if Serena would eventually turn out to be the stronger of the two players.

About a year earlier, Serena had had an accident that eventually caused her to change parts of her game—for the better. She'd been playing hooky from the private school she attended in Miami, skipping chemistry class to take a ride on her red skateboard. She wiped out on a sidewalk, breaking her fall by landing on her left wrist, and jammed it in the process. For weeks afterwards, she was unable to hit her favorite stroke, the two-handed backhand, without feeling some pain. This forced Serena (a righty) to concentrate on

developing power and accuracy with her forehand—
a new strength that would eventually make the
difference in several of her coming victories.

Traveling to Paris with Oracene in February 1999,
Serena worked her way up through the rounds of the
Gaz de France, then defeated Frenchwoman Amelie
Mauresmo in a long, thrilling final match. Serena
won the first set 6–2, then dropped her lead by losing
the second set 3–6. But she came back and fought
hard, winning seven out of four points in a tiebreaker
to end the final set, 7–6. There had been lots of talk
of Mauresmo's muscular shoulders last year when she
played in the finals of the Australian Open, but after
the Paris final, the consensus was that Serena's
bulging arms were much more defined—more "cut,"
as Serena liked to say. Serena had heard a lot about
her opponent's powerful strokes, but apparently the
French player was nowhere near as strong as Venus,
Serena's main practice partner. "I don't think that
[Mauresmo] hit that hard," she told reporters after the
match. "Maybe I am just used to it." In any case,
through a combination of pure muscle power and
smart playing, Serena prevailed.

It was her first professional singles title. (She and
Venus had won a doubles title previously.) With her win
in Paris, Serena moved up to No. 21. "I'm really proud of
myself, the way I handled the crowd and the way I came
back at the end. It's the best day of my career."

Serena e-mailed Venus, who was excited to hear
the news, but also a little sad to have missed the
event in person. Venus felt she had to live up to what
Serena had done, so a few hours later at the IGA
Classic in Oklahoma City, big sister went in and
defended her title, beating South Africa's Amanda
Coetzer in two sets. Venus dominated the game so
well that the second set lasted only 21 minutes.
"I found out [Serena] won and I really felt that it
was my duty to come out and win," Venus later said.
Venus had played a perfect tournament—she had

Steffi Graf of Germany smashes a forehand to Venus during a match at the 1999 Sydney International Tennis Tournament, which Graf won. A 21-time Grand Slam winner, Graf was once ranked number one for a record 377 weeks.

not lost a single set during the entire event.

Asked what it was like to have both daughters achieve titles on the same day, Richard Williams said, "I felt like crying. To have two daughters win on the same day means a lot." Serena's win also gave Richard a chance to talk up his youngest daughter, who didn't always receive the same press attention as Venus. "I don't think anyone challenges the ball like Serena does. . . . No one hits a forehand like Serena. No one takes control of a serve as well as Serena."

Jubilant as he was, Richard was still quick to put his girls' successes in perspective: "Even if they didn't win, I felt like they were winners for coming so far." After all, tennis was just one part of the girls' lives— and a part that would eventually end. Unlike his daughters, Richard said, too many young tennis players were not educating themselves, not preparing for their futures after tennis:

> In my mind, I just wish these kids would go out and get an education and use it. Play tennis, go to college, and then go off and do something. Be an astronaut, be a mayor, be a teacher. They aren't opening books. All they do is get done playing tennis, and then come right back to it. All they want to do is get a job coaching, or get on TV as a commentator. Don't they get tired of doing the same thing they've been doing since they were 4 years old?

The girls already like to talk about what they'd do when they retire from tennis, sometimes teasing the press by hinting that their last professional tournaments are just around the corner. Before moving on to the next field they plan to conquer, however, Serena and Venus still have plenty of goals to accomplish in tennis. In March 1999, Serena got a chance to redeem herself against Steffi Graf at the Evert Cup final. Before the match, Serena told reporters she wasn't intimidated by the older player—in words that exuded a bold ultra-confidence just like her older sister's. "I've never been intimidated by anyone, and unless I'm across the net from someone who's 10 feet tall and green, I won't be. On the other hand, because of my size and skills, I can intimidate anyone."

With Venus watching from the stands (she had chosen not to play any singles at this event), Serena opened her game against Steffi strongly, faltered during the second set, but then took command again of the third set to beat the German superstar. Serena prevailed even though she was suffering from a knee injury. After the game, Graf conceded she'd lost because her opponent played a more aggressive game and took more risks.

By this point, Serena, now ranked at No. 16, was feeling even more self-assured than usual. "I'm tired of losing to people I should beat. Whatever my potential is, I want to reach it—now. And if I do,

I see Venus as my biggest competition."

For the early part of the year, the Williams family seemed to have adopted a strategy of "divide and conquer" with each sister playing separate tournaments. The aim was to avoid putting the girls—and the whole Williams household—under too much pressure. But now it was beginning to look as if an on-court meeting was inevitable. The press began to compare the two players, noting that 17-year-old Serena was more outgoing and friendly off the court than 18-year-old Venus, but had a meaner game face and made little effort to bond with other players. "I'd prefer it for people to regard me as unapproachable," Serena told reporters. Venus had the faster serve, observers noted, but Serena's was more consistently powerful. Venus had the better backhand, Serena the better forehand. And because of her longer experience on the tour, observers speculated, Venus was probably mentally tougher during competition. But everyone agreed, both girls had been playing exceptionally well this season.

The Lipton Championships in late March gave the sisters their first shot at playing against each other since the Australian Open the previous year. During early rounds, Venus, ranked No. 3 in the world, struggled quite a bit to keep her lead, but eventually won in the quarterfinals against a German player named Anke Huber. She then showed a new dimension to her game by playing a very patient, thoughtful game against Steffi Graf, waiting for the older player to make mistakes and using those openings to overpower her. Serena, meanwhile, ripped through the early rounds, powering over the former world number one player Monica Seles in two sets. She then defeated the Williams family "nemesis," Martina Hingis, by using a variety of shots and keeping the Swiss teen guessing. "I've worked really hard all my life since I was four years old," Serena said. "There comes a time you have to start winning. All my hard work is finally paying off."

Venus and Serena faced each other at the Lipton

finals on March 28, 1999. Much as they loved and supported each other, it was time to act like competitors. Venus spoke for both sisters when she said, "It's difficult to play against your sister. . . . But whoever I play—I play to win." Still, the girls tried to keep everything in perspective. No matter what happened, Serena told TV reporters, "In the end, we go home, we live life, and you have to be happy after that. So you have to remind yourself it's a game, and there's only one winner. And, of course, next week, there will be another opportunity."

During the match, Richard Williams held up a hand-lettered sign on a piece of cardboard, announcing to the world: "Welcome to the Williams show." Both players started out strong and slugged it out over three sets. They played their hardest, but it was impossible to completely forget that they were playing each other. Venus didn't celebrate or show any emotion on her face, even when Serena made errors. Serena got so frustrated at one point in the second set that she flung her racket across the court. Eventually, the older sister prevailed. They met at the net, exchanged high fives, and then Venus put her arm around Serena as they walked slowly off the court. Although they must have had tremendously mixed feelings at the time, they mustered a lot of grace, good sportsmanship, and love for one another at their press conference.

"It's so great Serena is doing so well," Venus said.

"Venus played a great match," Serena countered. "It was very exciting. I'm glad I was able to come back from [behind] and make it more interesting."

Serena proved herself to be a gracious loser to her big sister—but in just a few months, she'd get another chance to face her toughest opponent. Both girls experienced disappointing losses in the singles tournament at the French Open in June and were eliminated in the first week—losing to older, wiser opponents. But there they did win their first Grand Slam women's doubles title—defeating Martina Hingis and Anna Kournikova

—and became only the second sister team to win a Grand Slam doubles event since 1890, when Ellen and Grace Roosevelt won what is now called the U.S. Open.

Venus and Serena then began gearing up for the two late-season major events, Wimbledon and the U.S. Open. Serena spoke with great enthusiasm about her chances at Wimbledon, and even talked about the great formal dresses she owned that she'd like to wear one day to the traditional Wimbledon ball. But just four days before the classic English event, Serena pulled out of the competition, saying she was sick with the flu.

The sports press smelled something fishy. Was Serena really ill, or was this some kind of ploy on the part of the crafty Williams family? Was Serena pulling out just so she wouldn't have to face her sister again, or maybe to give Venus a chance to reach the finals without competition from her younger sibling? Martina Navratilova— a former tennis superstar and now a ubiquitous commentator—fanned the flames for conspiracy-minded observers when she told newspapers, "You don't withdraw on a Thursday when you may not have to play until Tuesday or Wednesday of the next week. Either Serena had another injury or didn't want to play against Venus for whatever reason. I just wish they would tell the truth, because flu is not the truth."

Over the years, Richard Williams and his daughters had been at the center of plenty of minor sports controversies. Because they mostly kept to themselves, occasionally said inflammatory or colorful things to the press, and generally preferred to do things their own way, the Williams family had always been enveloped by a certain mystique. Outside the family, you never knew for sure what they were thinking or planning. This mystique only made reporters and fans all the more hungry for speculation about the Williamses' actions and motives.

So there were plenty of theories about Serena's absence at Wimbledon. And it did seem plausible

Venus Williams (foreground) and Serena are formidable doubles opponents as well as hitting partners.

that the Williams were managing the careers of the two girls in such a way to keep them from having to compete with each other too often, and to give each girl a chance to win and move up the ranks. Rarely did the two girls play in the same singles events other than the Grand Slam tournaments. But outside the immediate family circle, the details of the Williams family strategy would probably never be known. Meanwhile, the two young superstars paid no heed to the flap in the press, and continued to play the best tennis of their lives so far.

In September 1999, Venus—now 19—was defeated in the U.S. Open semifinals by Martina Hingis, who had remained her number one rival. But Serena was still in the event, and faced Martina in a later round. Even before the match, there was a minor bit of off-court warfare between Hingis and the Williams family, with a few insults being passed back and forth in the press. Richard Williams told reporters he thought Hingis was scared of Serena; Hingis responded by denying any fear and calling the Williams family a bunch of "big mouths." Soon afterwards, Serena shot back by calling Hingis uneducated.

By the time of the match, these incidents had been publicly forgiven and (theoretically) forgotten—but once they were on-court, the two opponents got a chance to work out all their aggression against one another. In the end, Serena's power prevailed over Martina's more strategic, cautious game. Serena made lots of unforced errors—57 in total—while Hingis made only 24; but Serena hit a whopping 36 winning points compared to Martina's meager 7.

It was the little sister's day of triumph. Serena Williams was the U.S. Open champion, and her ranking now shot up to No. 4 in the world. Some newspapers claimed that she was actually the best player in the world, despite the three competitors (Venus, Martina, and Lindsay Davenport) who out-ranked her.

During her stellar 1999 season, Serena hadn't won a single finals game against Venus. Yet now she was the first of the Williams girls to win a singles title in a Grand Slam event—an honor that her older sister had sought for years. Did this unexpected event make Venus a little bit jealous, a little bit anxious to try to regain the advantage of her position as the older, more experienced sister? Much as Venus loves her kid sis, doesn't Serena represent a perpetual challenge—an opponent just as strong as Venus, nearly as tall, and potentially as skilled?

Serena and sister Venus sport milk mustaches in this advertisement. The sisters also promote seatbelt usage and other public issues.

During Serena's finals match, Venus sat under a concealing, black hooded sweatshirt, her arms crossed defensively in a position that some observers interpreted as a sign of disappointment and envy.

It seems only natural that the successes of one sibling make the other one work harder to prevail, even if there's a lot of love and cooperation between them. But the world probably won't know for sure until one day in the future, when Venus, Serena, Richard, or all three of them decide to publish their tennis memoirs.

9

DREAMS ACHIEVED,
DREAMS ANTICIPATED

Venus proudly hugs the women's singles trophy at Wimbledon in July 2000 after defeating Lindsay Davenport in the finals. Venus was the first African American to win the Wimbledon title since Arthur Ashe in 1975, and the first black woman since Althea Gibson in 1958.

VENUS HOPED TO get her shot at a Grand Slam title in early 2000. But tendonitis in both her wrists left her unable to play in the Australian Open in January. Richard began talking to the press about her possible retirement, noting that she had really fallen in love with her fashion design courses at an arts college in Fort Lauderdale. She'd also been dabbling on the Internet, thinking about Web site development, dreaming of entrepreneurial success. Perhaps the number one spot in women's tennis—still strongly defended by Martina Hingis—didn't seem as important a goal for Venus, now that she could envision a bright future in a different field altogether.

Even Serena, her father hinted, was thinking about walking away from the game when her contract with Puma expired in three years. The early retirement of his daughters could serve as a statement, Richard explained. "I've seen too many black athletes come out of the ghetto and earn all that money, and four or five years later they're broke and no one cares who they once were. Because of the planning we've done with these two girls, they don't need tennis anymore."

But would the self-assured, trash-talking, boastful Venus really give up on tennis even before bringing home a Grand Slam title? Some reporters figured the Williams family was simply up to its usual mischief in the press, taunting fans with talk of retirement. When asked about her sister's long break from the game, Serena giggled and said, "I have the inside information. Unfortunately, I'm not able to release that." Later in the same interview, she joked, "I'm going to announce my retirement at Wimbledon." She then corrected herself, saying, "This is my last event. It's been swell."

All this joshing around couldn't completely hide the fact that both Venus and Serena were suffering from various injuries and losing their edge. Venus, ranked No. 3 in December, slipped to No. 5 by June, while Serena dropped from No. 4 to No. 8. But at Wimbledon, Serena made it to the third round and played fiercely against Yvette Basting of the Netherlands, taking two sets in a mere 35 minutes. Basting won only one game out of the entire 13-game match. Venus, now 20 years old, also won, against Ai Sugiyama from Japan. In the next round both girls prevailed, with Venus beating her rival, the top-ranked Hingis, so badly that the Swiss teenager later mourned, "Someone else probably deserves to be Number 1."

The Williams girls then faced each other in the semifinals—and once again, Venus prevailed, although she didn't seem very happy to have to eliminate her beloved sister. Richard Williams was so distraught, he didn't even attend the sisterly showdown. "It's really bitter," Venus said after winning. "But someone had to move on." (Conspiratorial observers suggested that Serena had thrown the game on purpose to give Venus a shot at the title—a charge that Richard vehemently denied.)

Big sister then went on to face Lindsay Davenport in the final. Venus was in prime form. She swooped and grunted and lunged after the ball, and came at the defending champion with serves so powerful, they sounded like ropes being snapped. She demolished Davenport in two sets. Finally, Venus had the Grand Slam title she'd been preparing for all these years.

She laughed and leaped around on the grass, then climbed into her family's box. The sisters put their

heads together and whispered joyously. Richard Williams, meanwhile, jumped out on top of the NBC booth and started dancing around. Chris Evert, a commentator sitting inside the booth, thought the roof was going to come down.

"All my life I've dreamed of winning a Grand Slam, and when I wake up it's a nightmare," Venus said after the match. "I don't have to wake up like that anymore."

Venus was the first African American to win a Wimbledon title since Arthur Ashe in 1975, and the first black women since Althea Gibson in 1958. It was a good thing she was prepared—a week before the event, she'd gone out and purchased a gown for the Wimbledon ball.

Richard Williams (left) celebrates with Serena and business manager Leland Hardy (right) after Venus wins the women's singles championship at Wimbledon in July 2000. Venus took the match against defending champion Lindsay Davenport in a thrilling tiebreaker.

A few months later, Venus would pick up her second major title at the U.S. Open. Wearing a vibrant orange sherbet halter dress, a sparkling choker, and shimmering earrings, Venus came out into the Arthur Ashe Stadium on September 9, 2000, and won another audacious victory against fellow American Lindsay Davenport. The Williams family broke out in jubilation. Richard, always a hound for the spotlight, came out and walked his daughter back onto the court as the crowd cheered. He then started dancing around and pointing to the sky, just a few feet from where a disheartened Davenport sat in her sideline chair.

Richard Williams was too busy celebrating to be polite. After all, his daughter had made good on her 10-year-old promise to reach the pinnacles of tennis success. True, she wasn't yet ranked number one, but she was a two-time Grand Slam champion. Her sister trailed just a bit behind. And as a team, they were already unstoppable. They had already changed the way tennis was played and watched, and had brought a sense of excitement and drama—yes, even a little soap opera, given all their verbal battles with Martina and other players—back into the game. Venus was now arguably the highest-profile athlete in the world next to fellow barrier-breaker, Tiger Woods.

Asked after the U.S. Open if she thought her No. 3 ranking was inaccurate, Venus crowed, "Oh, yeah. Oh, yeah. I feel very good. I've always felt like the best player."

Since girlhood, Venus Williams has received a lot of attention for her natural athletic abilities at track, tennis, and other endeavors—abilities she no doubt inherited from her father, who was also very gifted at a number of sports. (Remember, tennis coach Rick Macci was almost more impressed with Venus's spontaneous back-flips and ability to walk on her hands than with her hitting.) But "nature" is only one part of the story. Nature gives certain individuals some great advantages over other athletes: the potential for greater strength, speed, and endurance. Without the willingness to work hard and build upon nature, however, people just coasting on their "potential" are relying on luck to get where they want to be.

Most of Venus's potential clearly lies in her strength and her power. When people focus on these gifts, do they shortchange Venus's intelligence, will, and hard work? Some close observers of the tennis scene would say so. They've noticed how reporters and commentators always seem to remark on Venus's "power," sometimes even comparing her aggressiveness to that of a "caged animal," while highlighting the intelligence or "cerebral nature" of white players like Davenport or Hingis.

Of course, there is some justification for such contrasts. Hingis, for example, has always been an exceptionally perceptive player, using her skills, accuracy, and intuition to dominate players with more physical strength. And in her earliest encounters with professional players, Venus certainly let her size, strength, and speed do most of the work for her: she would win a lot of points, but make many unforced errors in the process. But according to some fans and knowledgeable observers, Venus over the years has become a tremendously "cerebral" player as well.

During one of her matches, John McEnroe—who was always known as a "bad boy" of tennis, but was progressive enough in his racial politics to refuse to play in South Africa during the apartheid era—told the TV audience, "Venus works extremely hard at her game. The other day, she played [Natalie] Tauziat three tough sets, then played a doubles match and then was out on the practice court that night—all in the same day." It was a welcome acknowledgement, especially coming from a commentator who'd previously focused on criticizing Venus and Serena for their apparent unfriendliness.

Eric Riley, a renowned African-American tennis coach in Philadelphia, has always seen the Williams' success on the court as an intellectual achievement. Playing aggressively, going for your shots, aiming for the lines at every opportunity, refusing to play it safe—these, according to Riley, are thought-out strategies, triumphs of mind over matter. First and foremost, Venus and Serena Williams have put their minds to the task of winning; their bodies are merely following orders. Riley believes that black athletes do have a tendency to play differently—with a more aggressive style—than their white colleagues, but the reasons are environmental rather than genetic or racial. "Coming up, you just knew that a passive person of color wouldn't make it [in a sport like tennis]," he says.

"I remember in the '60s and '70s, how it was believed that black men couldn't quarterback a football team because we weren't cerebral enough and didn't have leadership qualities," Riley says. "That wasn't true, and everybody knows it now. But football had a Doug Williams, a Randall Cunningham. Tennis still hasn't had to deal with a lot of African Americans excelling at the sport."

But now that Venus and Serena are here, there's a great chance all that will change—although it won't happen overnight. At the 1999 Advanta Championships in Philadelphia, Eric Riley noted that there were little black girls with beads in their hair everywhere in the audience when Venus was playing. But when Hingis played against Davenport later in the finals of that event, the crowd reverted to being predominantly white.

"Tennis has always been a game defined by Whiteness," was how writer Joy Duckett Cain described the game's history. "European players whose names sound of fjords and ice caps, Clorox-clean tennis togs, the blinding colorless summer sun, the pale fans sipping water and vodka tonics. In this crowd, Black players like Althea Gibson in the 1950's, Arthur Ashe in the 1960's and 1970's, and Zina Garrison in the 1980's and 1990's stood alone."

Venus and Serena Williams are still, to a great extent, a novelty act in the world of tennis. They dominate the sport in terms of publicity and earnings, but they are still among a small handful of nonwhite players who've achieved the highest ranks and titles. They thus run the risk of being "used" by others for their political and cultural value. As sports sociologist Jay Coakley has noted,

A bus parked in front of the Arthur Ashe Stadium, located in the Queens borough of New York City, features an image of Venus. Today, the tennis star and her sister continue the legacies that black stars like Arthur Ashe and Althea Gibson began.

> Tennis and golf and other traditional white sports are hungry to prove they are no longer racist. Golf has welcomed Tiger Woods with open arms because golf clubs have had to cope with the legacy that they have been exclusively for the wealthy white male. . . . The Williams sisters have done more to distance themselves from a legacy of racism in tennis than anyone else. . . . Corporations have done an exorbitant amount of market research that certain segments of the white population are hungry to demonstrate that they are not racist.

For many people, then, rooting for Venus and Serena is a way to enjoy the sport they love while defying its long, exclusionary history. Sports promoters and clothing manufacturers have been taking advantage of that fact from the day they first started pursuing young Venus for endorsement deals and competitive events. A different kind of personality might be angry about having to take on such a role. After all, the responsibility of athletes is to play their game as well as they can—not necessarily to make other people feel good about themselves, to help others "prove" that they're not racist, or to enable big, rich companies to become even bigger and richer. But neither Venus nor Serena seems unhappy about the role she's been given. When Serena was asked if she wished people would stop calling her a great *black* tennis player, and simply refer to her as a great tennis player, she blithely shrugged off the implication of the question. "I've never felt that way because I *am* black and kids look up to me, and I'm proud of that." No doubt Venus would respond similarly.

Over the years, there have been good and not-so-good episodes in the Williams sisters' unfolding Cinderella stories. Among the highlights have been major tournament wins, Olympic gold medals, lucrative endorsement deals, "revolutionary" multicolored on-court wardrobes, and nearly constant and mostly positive attention from the sports press. Among the low points were unexpected losses and boastful predictions that didn't come true. Bitter rivalries with other top women players. Racial epithets murmured on the court. Rumors about jealousy and competition between the two sisters. Accusations that the Williams sisters are arrogant and unfriendly, and that their father is a loose cannon who says all sorts of inappropriate things in public.

As black girls who grew up on the hard streets of Compton, Venus and Serena are still extremely notable exceptions in their field, and will always be remembered that way. But unlike their predecessors who walked this difficult path—unlike Gibson, Ashe, and Garrison—they do not have to stand alone. They are sisters who love their families and each other, and that is permanent.

CHRONOLOGY

1980   Venus Ebone Starr Williams is born to Richard and Oracene Williams on June 17 in Lynwood, California

1984   Richard Williams teaches himself tennis and begins coaching his fourth daughter, Venus, on the rough courts of South Central Los Angeles

1990   Venus becomes top-ranked player in the 12-and-under category in southern California; national magazines and newspapers begin to profile her

1991   Moves with family to Orlando, Florida, and enrolls in Richard Macci's tennis academy

1994   Turns pro at the age of 14; at the instruction of her parents and the WTA plays a limited number of tournaments each year

1995   Signs a $12-million endorsement deal with Reebok; the family moves to Palm Beach Gardens estate; Richard Williams takes over as coach again

1997   Venus graduates from high school and starts taking fashion design and other classes at local arts college

1998   Wins her first professional event, mixed doubles at Australian Open; takes first singles title at IGA Classic; defeats Serena in their first professional showdown; is ranked No. 5 at the end of season

1999   Successfully defends IGA Classic title; on the same day, Serena wins her first professional tournament; Venus beats Serena again at the Lipton finals, lifting her to No. 3; Serena wins Wimbledon title, her first Grand Slam, before Venus does

2000   Venus comes back from injuries to win her first and second Grand Slam titles at Wimbledon and U.S. Open

2001   With sister Serena wins the doubles Australian Open Grand Slam; Venus clinches her second Wimbledon title

TOURNAMENT STATS

(Adapted from Sanex WTA Tour Media Information System)

YEAR	DATE	EVENT	PRIZE	RANK
1994	November 6	Oakland	$5,350	0
1995	August 13	Los Angeles	$1295	0
	August 20	Canadian Open	$2175	0
	November 5	Oakland	$10,215	321
1996	March 17	Indian Wells	$1,500	217
	April 14	Amelia Island	$1,285	197
	August 18	Los Angeles	$4,215	192
	August 25	San Diego	$2.600	148
	November 10	Oakland	$3,150	207
1997	March 16	Indian Wells	$20,500	211
	April 13	Amelia Island	$2,150	102
	June 8	French Open	$14,520	90
	July 6	Wimbledon	$7,701	59
	August 10	Los Angeles	$4,950	59
	September 7	U.S. Open	$350,000	66
	October 19	Zurich (Switzerland)	$16,875	26
	November 2	Moscow (Russia)	$16,875	24
1998	January 18	Sydney (Australia)	$26,500	21
	February 1	Australian Open	$55,667	16
	March 1	*Oklahoma City	$27,200	14
	March 15	Indian Wells	$41,750	12
	March 29	*Lipton	$235,000	11
	May 10	Italian Open (Rome)	$60,000	9
	June 7	French Open	$75,700	7
	July 5	Wimbledon	$78,961	6
	August 2	Stanford	$36,000	5
	September 13	U.S. Open	$200,000	5
	October 4	*Grand Slam Cup (Germany)	$662,400	5
	October 18	Zurich	$67,500	5

YEAR	DATE	EVENT	PRIZE	RANK
1999	January 31	Australian Open	$47,402	6
	February 21	Hanover (Germany)	$40,000	6
	February 28	*Oklahoma City	$27,000	5
	March 28	*Lipton	$265,500	6
	May 2	*Hamburg (Germany)	$80,000	7
	May 9	*Italian Open	$150,000	5
	June 6	French Open	$38,347	5
	July 4	Wimbledon	$75,415	5
	August 8	San Diego	$40,000	4
	September 10	U.S. Open	$80,000	3
2000	July 11	French Open	$76,472	4
	July 30	*Stanford	$87,000	3
	August 6	*San Diego	$87,000	3
	August 27	New Haven	$87,000	3
	September 10	*U.S. Open	$800,000	3
	October 22	Linz	$43,500	3
2001	January 28	Australian Open	$115,875	3
	February 18	Nice	$22,500	3
	March 18	Indian Wells	$59,250	3
	March 23	*Ericcson Open	$2,720,000	3
	April 30	*Hamburg	$565,000	3

*Won tournament title

BIBLIOGRAPHY

Books and Periodicals

Aronson, Virginia. *Venus Williams*. Philadelphia: Chelsea House Publishers, 1999.

———. *Venus & Serena Williams*. Philadelphia: Chelsea House Publishers, 2001.

Friedman, Devin. "Sister Act." *Elle Magazine*, January 2001.

Gibson, Althea. *I Always Wanted to Be Somebody*. New York: Harper & Brothers, 1958.

Johnson, Anne Jannette. *Great Women in Sports*. Detroit: Visible Ink Press, 1996.

King, Billie Jean, and Cynthia Starr. *We Have Come a Long Way: The Story of Women's Tennis*. New York: McGraw-Hill Book Company, 1988.

Mewshaw, Michael. *Ladies of the Court*. New York: Crown Publishers, 1993.

Price, S.L. "Point After: Spoiled Sport Amid the Pomp of the U.S. Open." *Sports Illustrated*, September 8, 1997.

Teitlebaum, Michael. *Grand Slam Starts: Martina Hingis and Venus Williams*. New York: Harper Active, 1998.

BIBLIOGRAPHY

Websites

Venus and Serena Williams
http://www.thewilliamssisters.net

Arthur Ashe Tribute
http://www.cnnsi.com/tennis/features/1997/arthurashe/

American Tennis Association
http://www.atanational.com

Venus Page of the WTA Tour Page
http://64.157.1.99/players/player_bio.asp?PlayerBio=Williams_Venus%2Ehtm

INDEX

———— ❦ ————

INDEX

———— ❧ ————

INDEX

PICTURE CREDITS

SANDY ASIRVATHAM, a graduate of Columbia University with a B.A. in philosophy and economics and a M.F.A. in writing, is a journalist, creative writer, and aspiring musician living in Baltimore. As a professional writer for more than 10 years, she has written extensively about business, government, and the arts. Her other books for Chelsea House include a biography of Bruce Willis, a history of the police in America, and an examination of the late 17th-century Salem witch trials. This is her first book on a sports subject.